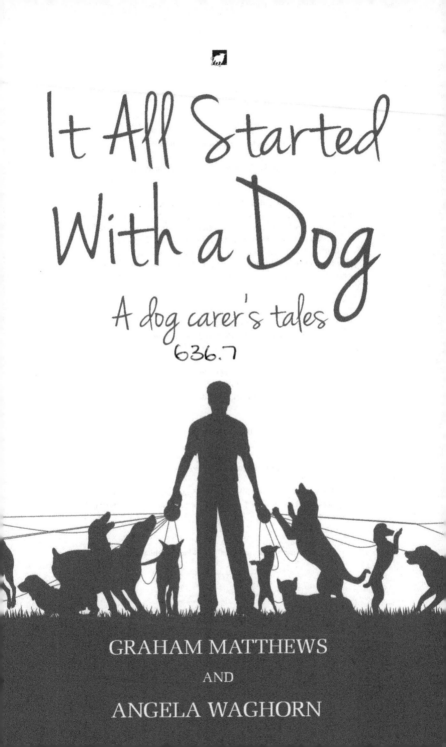

It All Started With a Dog

A dog carer's tales

636.7

GRAHAM MATTHEWS

AND

ANGELA WAGHORN

Matador
9 Priory Business Park,
Wistow Road, Kibworth Beauchamp,
Leicestershire. LE8 0RX
Tel: 0116 279 2299
Email: books@troubador.co.uk
Web: www.troubador.co.uk/matador
Twitter: @matadorbooks

ISBN 978 1784624 477

British Library Cataloguing in Publication Data.
A catalogue record for this book is available from the British Library.

Printed and bound by CPI Group (UK) Ltd, Croydon, CR0 4YY
Typeset in 11pt Aldine401 BT by Troubador Publishing Ltd, Leicester, UK

Matador is an imprint of Troubador Publishing Ltd

*To my beautiful wife Angela
without whom this book would
not have been possible*

It all started with a dog! Nero in fact was a trainee guide dog for the blind. I had signed up as a puppy walker, and being a single parent and male they gave me the biggest dog they had (paws like a lion). That dog managed to get me into so many tight corners it was untrue.

During his church training I arrived late and sneaked in at the back pew putting Nero underneath the pew. Nero being well trained by now duly went to sleep. The dried food supplied by the Guide Dog Association worked its magic and Nero let go of the biggest silent fart you can imagine. As the fart bounced its way down the aisle to the altar, each row in turn turned in my direction. They called themselves Christians but the looks I received were very unfriendly. I couldn't stand up in the middle of a service and declare the fart was the unseen dogs responsibility.

How can a dog make you look stupid? Simple: ask a cinema manager if you can bring a guide dog into his establishment for free as part of his training. Then wait for the manager's reply explaining that not many blind people frequent cinemas to watch films.

During his early training Nero had a problem with small children. He wasn't aggressive just clumsy in his attempts to play with them. The fat controller from the Guide Dog Association suggested I take him around to the local school at playtime. This, it was hoped, would get Nero used to children's play and jerky erratic movements. Being a middle-aged man I first checked with the school office and received agreement that I could stand outside the school fence during playtime. The next day within five minutes of standing at the fence a male teacher challenged my purpose in being there, I always remember a warm glow about that knowing that the local kids were being well looked after. I reiterated this story to a neighbour of mine who had two boys at the school. She very kindly offered to walk Nero around to the school when collecting her boys as part of Nero's training.

On her return with Nero she announced she had arranged for me to take him to her son's class. The following day I gave a talk to three separate classes on what it was like to have a guide dog. I hadn't realised what I'd let myself in for. A few days later I received a thank you card signed by all the children and felt very proud and humble at the same time. My neighbour and I have remained friends ever since to the extent she dropped her two lads off with me saying she had had enough and I looked after them for the day while she had respite. This is an example both of how people automatically trust guide dog owners and how a guide dog can open doors and help you make friends with people you wouldn't ordinarily meet.

Nero as mentioned before was a big dog with an appetite to match. As such he was always being put on an involuntary diet. It became so bad that he looked down at his food bowl one day and then looked at me with accusing eyes. What could I do! Nero however had a plan. Pebble dashing, tree bark and grazing like a herbivore were suddenly on the menu. Three months later the sixty foot tree, devoid of lower bark, crashed down narrowly missing the house. The bald patch of pebble dashing has been left like a blue plaque to Nero's presence.

Nero's diet caused me a few academic problems as well. Apart from being a single parent and puppy walker I'd also embarked on an undergraduate's course. I was sent various specimens which I kept on a large wooden box in the front room called a television. I needed to refer to the specimen of a pig's heart partly cut away and impregnated to preserve it, but couldn't find the heart on the box. I then went on a search of the entire house with an intensity that the British Heart Foundation would have been proud of. I eventually found the pig's heart halfway down the garden in Nero's mouth. Nero had decided to supplement his meagre rations with my specimen of a mammalian bi-valve heart. Eventually I returned the specimen back to the university with a note saying the blind dog did it . I never heard any more regarding the teeth marks in the pig's heart.

Nero affected my studies in other ways as the university administration became aware I had a guide dog. I started to receive course work in extra large print so the guide and reference notes I received never tied up with the reference and book page numbers. The disabilities officer at each university I studied at would pull me aside in front of the whole class to check if I was okay, and see if I required extra help. At exam time I was always offered extra time because of my blind disability.

Nero's unusual dietary supplements had side effects. His toilet became somewhat unpredictable. One day at the Tesco weekly shop (8 am Friday to avoid the mad cow rush) he shit. A mistake certainly but the woman who screamed in horror had surely lead a sheltered life. My willy hanging out would have caused less fuss. It was all the fault of the dead squirrel Nero on his twice-weekly run ate the dead squirrel and refused to come back as he hadn't yet managed to swallow the tail. To see your dog running around with a squirrel's tail hanging out of its mouth is somewhat horrifying, the primeval experience sent a shiver down my spine.

Having experienced this I was somewhat concerned about Nero's biological functions. Whilst trying to toilet Nero in the kerb prior to his pub training (he needed lots of pub training), a man grabbed me by the arm and took me across the road. Being embarrassed for the man I foolishly pretended to be blind and then returned to my journey to the pub. No, the man returned to assure me I was going in the wrong direction and put me on the right path. Eventually I reached the pub. Nero was well known in the pub, all the customers knew his name, me I was just known as Nero's dad. The dog received a bowl of water long before I was served with a pint.

Nero's training had its upsides of course. Like when I took him for crowd training at the local dog track. A man who worked for one of the betting chains took pity on me because of the guide dog. Every tip he gave me won. It started with a fiver and quickly escalated to fifty pound bets. The money I won paid in part for the dog-training expenses. Not being a greedy man when the dog left I never went dog racing again.

A curious thing happened whilst walking Nero in the woods one day. I came across a group of people who were standing by a tree trunk looking intently down. To my horror I discovered they were all looking at a snake and Nero was trying to sniff the snake's head. The police had been called and duly turned up, but the two officers never came within ten yards of the snake.

The police radio crackled, the Sergeant at H.Q. was saying don't touch the snake, it's against the law to interfere with an indigenous species of snake. The two officers, now looking somewhat relieved, said "don't worry sarge we will clear the area and leave the snake alone". Imagine the officers' horror when I mentioned that the snake was not an indigenous species.

"What do you know?" asked one of the officers.

"Well I kept snakes as a child, and that snake is not one of the three native species".

"What do you think it is?" enquired one of the officers.

"I have no idea," I replied, "but if I was to hazard a guess, I'd say it was a young constrictor".

Radio crackles, "here sarge there's a snake expert here who says it's not native".

"Bring it back to the station," says sarge. Both officers now start backing off hoping the other will be brave enough to pick the snake up. Realizing the two officers plight I instructed them to find a box and trapped the snake's head with a forked stick. It was then and only then I realized how big the snake was as upon picking it up it curled around the entire length of my arm.

I eventually untangled the snake and dropped it in the cardboard box provided by the officers. The two scaredy-cat officers now checked back to H.Q. as heroes. "We've got it sarge".

Sarge in the meantime had had second thoughts! "Don't bring the snake back to the station" he screamed. The two heroes were elated, we risked ourselves for orders and we're bringing the snake back. Just to take the edge of our heroes' glory I happened to mention how awful it would be to find the box empty back at the station. As the two officers had half a shift still to do in that panda car, the point wasn't missed.

With a guide dog you find most people very accommodating and on occasions they go beyond the call of duty. On one of Nero's working walks we passed a highways lorry digging up the road, I paused so Nero would experience the noise and smell. The workman immediately called out "are you training that dog mate", and I confirmed I was. All of a sudden every pneumatic appliance on the lorry was connected and in use. Nero of course being well trained by now was looking as if he'd heard it all before and seemed more interested in a dog-end lying in the kerb. If you watch the television news or read newspapers it's easy to forget how many good people there are in the country.

The main difficulty with a guide dog is he becomes a local celebrity and you become an add on. Even today people I don't know ask after Nero and refer to me as Nero's dad. He's been dead for over ten years and I only had him for nine months. When Nero left for his advance training I was so upset that I never took on another guide dog. Well when you've been up all night with the dog throwing up at both ends, cleaning up and lying on the floor saying daddy wishes he could do it for you. Well that's not a dog but a family member. Nero's legacy lasted long after he had gone and it was an experience I wouldn't have missed for the world.

Training Nero had changed my way of life. A strict regime going to places and doing things I wouldn't normally do. The number of local people I was on speaking terms with had gone up one-hundred-fold. It had all of a sudden stopped. I became a shadow of my former self until my son who had realised my plight showed me an advert in the local paper.

DOG CARERS WANTED.
LOOK AFTER DOG IN YOUR OWN HOME, GOOD RATES OF PAY.

Well I'd been looking after a dog in my own home for free. The beauty of this system was I could give the dog back before I became too attached and be paid. How wrong can you be! Every dog has its own character and story (good and bad), and the pay never really covered damage to fixtures and fittings. Regardless of this the dogs turned a ghost house back into a vibrant home. Let me take you to some of the highs and lows of life with man's best friend.

The first dogs I looked after belonged to a Scottish lady who although living in southern England returned to Scotland for medical treatment. Something about better treatment or not understanding the language down south. Both her dogs were clean and perfectly okay despite being rescue dogs. However one of the dogs displayed unusual behaviour when I went to the toilet. The poor dog would cower whenever I reappeared, tail between the legs, head down and shaking with fear. After a few minutes the dog would settle down and sit on my lap or do all the normal doggy things.

When the owner returned I enquired about the dog's strange and worrying behaviour. It did occur to me the owner might think I'd been mistreating the dog. It turned out the poor dog's first owner before being rescued was an alcoholic. He went out the front door and when he came back it could be punches or kicks or pats. The dog had been conditioned to being fearful until it could establish what mood the owner was in. Just a second out of sight and the dog was terrified. I have never hit a dog (except once, comes later) so I had difficulty understanding how someone had treated my dog like this. Oh yes it was my dog where had all the non attachment gone? I was glad when the owner had gone so I could weep in private. I had a lot of rescue dogs after that.

Enter Sunny or as I called him (lots of nicknames now) Sunny the sod. Sunny of course was a rescue dog that had all the outward appearance of being normal. On the first day or rather night the dog disappeared. Chasing a fox was the probable cause and being new to the house was unable to find his way back. At 2-3 am I gave up looking for him for fear of being arrested in neighbours' gardens as a burglar or worse a peeping tom. The next morning

I awoke to find Sunny asleep on the front door mat and not dead in a gutter somewhere. My relief quickly turned to embarrassment when neighbours knocked to quietly enquire what was wrong with my dog as he had been howling and barking all night in an attempt to be let in. My bedroom is over the front door and I'm not deaf; I thus earned the dubious distinction of being the only person in the street not to be kept awake all night.

Sunny of course had a few more problems being a rescue dog, two court orders (all failed) against him suggest he wasn't your everyday dog. Sunny had major "issues" with small children, loud bangs and other dogs, bitches were okay. My kind of dog then! Reading between the lines I surmise Sunny had been attacked by other dogs when a pup before being rescued and now as an adult had learnt to attack first. I also deduced small children had probably attached fireworks to his tail consequently he would have no truck with them and wouldn't allow them near him.

Guy Fawkes Night and it's lead up were an absolute nightmare. Early evening usually saw Sunny crying and messing on the floor. Normally clean Sunny just wouldn't go out when fireworks were about. Bedtime was worse, no mess, he would position himself between me and the pillow shaking like a leaf. I had to endure sitting bolt upright in bed until half an hour after the last firework went off.

Sunny's owner was a very nice lady who had to go into hospital for surgery. Upon her discharge I decided she needed more rest and kept Sunny for another week free of charge. Mid-week I visited her to make sure she was okay and on the mend and to collect more food for Sunny. Standing in her garage in her dressing gown she suddenly said "give me a big kiss". My first thought was what the bloody hell is going to happen to me now. Knowing she was on medication I decided to placate her by stepping forward and giving her a quick peck on the cheek and then stood back sharply. The woman somewhat taken aback asked why I had just kissed her. It was then I did a re-run of what she had actually said and realised in actual fact she had said "give Sunny a big kiss from me". With the skill of a Don Juan or Casanova I extradited myself by saying I couldn't give Sunny a kiss from her without kissing her first. Thankfully she accepted this and was really quite pleased, I had my hearing checked the following week and thanked the lord I hadn't thought she'd said something else even more embarrassing. This is an example of how quick-witted a dog carer needs to be to escape a custodial sentence and how a dog can sometimes get you into involuntary trouble.

Sadly in old age Sunny lost interest in his aggressive side and allowed other dogs near him. I used to tell them that in Sunny's youth they'd all be mincemeat. One day while walking Sunny on his lead a young pretender came over (English pointer). Sunny had always preferred bigger dogs to vent his past anger on. I explained to the pointer's owner Sunny wasn't good with other dogs and he duly put the dog's lead on and led him away. You could sense the terrible-teen pointer was not happy with this situation as he kept looking around at Sunny. Sure enough an acre away the pointer was let off the lead and came running back. Sunny had seen all this and actually smiled, not snarled, smiled. He even wagged his tail to encourage closer contact. Just within range the terrible teen was taught a lesson in life as Sunny didn't hold back on his verbal abuse in the course of his lunge. I never saw the pointer again, he probably got agoraphobia. Sunny looked as if he'd had a great morning and all before breakfast. Sunny the sod you couldn't help love him especially when you understood his history.

Henry the Boxer wasn't a bad dog but he wasn't good. I looked after him when he was just six months old for five weeks. At that age and over time I became a pack elder and leader to him. I'm not ashamed to admit I love that dog and he loves me. Henry was a show dog in all but his nuts which hadn't descended and had to be removed. Being a large Boxer he had an unsettling effect on people and other dogs. Let me explain if you saw a scruffy man walking towards you with a gun in his hand you might cross the road or preferably run the other way. Boxers look a bit like a Kalashnikov AK-47 to other dogs, they have big heads which are as wide as their shoulders. All muscle and no fat they appear to other dogs as dangerous and capable of doing a lot of damage.

In truth Boxers are extremely good with people and children in particular. They are clumsy and can be relied upon to crash into you, trees or furniture whilst in pursuit of a squirrel or a ball. Male Boxers are usually fearless and won't give ground when threatened; because of Henry's physical presence other dogs were always threatening him to keep away. This worked whilst a pup but on maturity he was prone to retaliate first, in part to protect me. Henry having a damaged foot had for the most part to be kept on the lead. Walking uphill in the local wood the two hooligans approached at speed declaring their presence. The two hooligans were two big Alsatians who ran free in the wood threatening all other dogs and their owners. Occasionally being over excited and full of their own majesty they would bite.

I was seriously considering dropping Henry's lead and running, every man for a boat sort of thing. Then I noticed a curious thing, Henry had spread his back legs in readiness for the coming onslaught. I decided to stick with him, sure enough over the brow of the hill came the hooligans. Suddenly with Henry in view the hooligans decided they had made a terrible mistake. Breaking hard they resembled a cartoon as dust shot up and they turned and ran. Henry just let out a half woof that signified his contempt. The hooligans never came near me or my other dogs again, just in case.

As mentioned earlier over the years of dogs attacking him Henry developed the ploy of getting retaliation in first. Imagine my horror then when the good owners decided to get a Shih Tzu as a companion for Henry. A Shih Tzu would not make a decent sandwich for Henry, madness I thought. Henry came to stay with his brother Louis the Shih Tzu (Shih Tzu are zoos with no animals). How wrong can you be as Louis dominated Henry. All right at Louis's size he had to jump on chairs in order to bite Henry's ears and chops or risk being crushed as he dived under Henry's body to savage one of his paws. Henry looked all forlorn as any game he played with me was always interrupted by Louis.

Henry liked to spar with me, yes Boxers do actually box. In play I received a black eye, numerous cuts and bruises and a bloody nose plus a torrent of swearing (threatening growls). Boxers have very small peg like teeth and rely in the main on their physical strength to dominate the opposition. Louis however wishing to join in would use his needle like teeth to bite whatever part of your anatomy he could reach and hurt the most.

With Henry the fearless as your big brother you can punch well above your weight. Like the day next door's Alsatian dared bark at little Louis. Louis was straight over the garden fence and chased the disrespectful Alsatian back into his house. As in human life Louis was always going to be the last one to know that Henry wasn't his biological brother.

Henry became embroiled in a fight with an Airedale Terrier (they have big teeth). After a few days a flap of skin popped up around a puncture wound. Worried I took Henry to the vet. The vet explained the flap was just dead tissue and produced a pair of scissors. I requested gas and air to which the vet replied "the dog won't need it". I then explained it was for me as he snipped the flap off Henry's shoulder.

Being a dog person my name spread far and wide, well in my street it did. One night I sat down to watch a late night t.v. programme titled *Can you be a scientist and believe in God*. As a scientist I was interested and poured myself a large glass of wine when there was a knock at the door. A young attractive neighbour was knocking to ask for help with her cat who was stuck in the extension roof. Straight away I thought there is a god especially when she explained her husband was on nights. Five minutes later I was up a ladder in the pitch black night trying to catch her pussy. The same thing happened a year later. This time though a woman I was courting was less than pleased a young woman had knocked me up in the middle of the night to find her cat. Her husband knocked the following day to thank me and exclaimed "I hear you were on cat watch again last night".

The same woman (thank god she was attractive) got me into a scrape where I could have lost life and limb. It started with a strange noise, it wasn't human but sounded as if it might be, if that makes sense. The attractive neighbour called to me to please help. What had happened was another neighbour's dog had escaped. The big Rottweiler had pushed a fence aside to get out but couldn't push it back to get in. The owner worked in the security industry and obviously used the rotty as a guard dog. The rotty being a guard dog was none too pleased with people being on his patch. Even more annoying then to find a Dalmatian (brown spots). Rotty had managed to corner the Dalmatian who had suddenly realised he was on rotty's menu. The owner of the Dalmatian was a dumb woman hence the weird noise as she attempted to scream. I've never heard a noise like it before or since, it was the best she could manage in the circumstances.

Reluctantly I approached the Rottweiler, he gave me a sniff of approval as if to say let's share the Dalmatian. The poor dumb woman cowering over her dog was still making a strange noise. What a spectacle that was. The Dalmatian was deaf but nevertheless was aware the future was not looking that bright. I gave the Rottweiler a tickle behind the it's ear. It just looked at me. I then chanced two fingers under the dog's collar and led him away. Well most people can afford to lose two fingers but this dog was capable of taking a whole hand at least. The dumb woman and her deaf dog never thanked me; I don't suppose I would have understood what they were saying anyway.

What now to do now with the guard dog and still get my two collar fingers back intact. I simply broke back through the garden fence, through the back kitchen door, filled up the dog's water bowl patted rotty on the head and left. What kind of guard dog would you call that. The owner never thanked me either, in fact all the years he's lived diagonally opposite he's never spoken to us.

Dogs can get you into trouble just by their name without any form of aggression or threat. This was the case with a young medium-sized black staff, with a sweet nature especially with children. Whilst walking her in the park a young black boy walking towards me saw the dog and being a bit anxious he tried a different path. I called to the lad the dog was all right and friendly. The black lad continued to pass but the dog turned around to introduce herself to him. Realizing the lad's plight I called out Sooty come here. The black boy gave me a look that could have killed and I think some mention was made of the lad's father coming around to my house to break both my legs. Misunderstanding or not I let Sooty answer the door for the next few days.

Dogs can also get you out of trouble. Enter big Danny an English Mastiff who in his stockinged feet stood at over six feet and weighed ten stone. Danny was completely harmless, he wouldn't hurt a fly. The owner's house backed onto a park with a garden gate so at night I took him to the park. Technically the park was closed at night but a bunch of drunken yobs were having a drinks party there. They proceed to verbally abuse me saying I must be some kind of pervert, an old fogey because of my cap and pipe.

Out of the darkness and mist trotted Danny who was intent on greeting the yobs and engage in a spot of petting. When he passed me I called out to Danny "leave them". The yobs of course thought Danny was in attack mode and ran off. Some even managed to drop their beer cans. Danny looked very sad and couldn't understand why everyone had gone without even an hello or pat.

Danny did have a dark day once. On a walk one day he sniffed out a damaged, sick or diseased fox. Well he must have read a book or something because he snapped the fox's neck in under a second threw it into the air and snapped its back. Any other dog would have been okay so why the fox? Not content with his victory he ran home to show the household his mastiff powers. The household was a Russo/Greek mother and her two grown daughters. Danny was running around the house showing off his trophy the three females were also running around the house screaming with their hands on their heads. Eventually I managed to remove the fox from Danny and left the house to dispose of the fox. Upon my return the Greek mother had phoned her Russian MP husband in Russia who had informed her to keep her mouth shut as he knew it was a problem in England when a dog hunts a fox. After calming everyone down I explained that was the least of our problems. For big Danny to catch a fox the fox must have been seriously ill and Danny might have caught something. We took off in the owner's car as if it were an ambulance with the siren on.

Having just returned from Russia the Greek woman managed to take every roundabout the wrong way. The look of fear on people's faces coming the right way was unforgettable. Upon reaching the vet with the English mastiff, owned by a Russian Greek couple I discovered the vet was Italian. After lengthy slow explanations we eventually got there and the vet prescribed tablets and because of Danny's size he required three courses of three, £50 consultation and £80 for the tablets. If there is anything in reincarnation come back as a vet, they have shed loads of money. The journey back to Danny's house was equally frightening as not one roundabout was taken the right way, the only difference now was I didn't scream as much or as loud.

Mini Mouse wasn't good but he wasn't bad. A yorkie who was a rescue dog that had obviously had a very bad early life. The owner was a lovely French lady who had started off fostering Mini Mouse (being French she pronounced his name as Mini Moose), and had been conned by the rescue centre into keeping the dog. Mini Mouse had (in my opinion) been kicked in the head hard. As a consequence he had many medical disorders which were complicated over time. Brain damage, missing teeth, blind, deaf, incontinence and diabetes (two injections per day) were to visit that brave little dog over time. The owner was a saint to take him on and spent no small sum on his medication and diet.

The first time I had Mini Mouse I knew he was going to need special care. I went to bed early one night, I sleep the sleep of the just and innocent, nothing wakes me. In the middle of the night I awoke to find Mini Mouse sleeping peacefully next to my face. Not a problem for me but were was the beautiful woman who was supposed to be lying next to me? I found her sleeping in the spare bedroom. Now I'm no saint and thought at first we'd had a row. Being forgetful I struggled to think of what I had said or done and how many flowers or chocolates it would take to get back on an even keel. After much thought I realised I was innocent so I woke Angela enquiring "what are you doing here you silly cow". It then transpired that Mini Mouse had threatened her upon entry into the bedroom and wouldn't allow her anywhere near the bed. I slept all the way through this battle of wills but was now aware that Mini Mouse's behaviour could impact upon my naturals.

Eventually and in a very rapid space of time I persuaded Mini Mouse to sleep by the side of the bed and allow as many people to sleep in the bed as was possible (well two at most). Mini Mouse could when required metamorphose into a lion. Yorkies being terriers can adopt a ferocious demeanour. Unsighted as he was Mini couldn't allow other dogs to play the chase game with him. Simply he couldn't see them coming and would get knocked over. It didn't matter whether a dog was very large or small two fingers from Mini Mouse the lion was enough to send them packing. Mini Mouse's antisocial behaviour was not just restricted to other dogs. Not being prejudiced he would also threaten people or rather a certain aspect of people's bodies namely their feet. Well let's face it if you have had half your teeth kicked out and suffered brain damage you might develop a reflex action around people's feet. Mini Mouse would attack anyone's feet if he perceived a kick coming his way out of the gloom of his eyesight. No open-toed shoes or sandals near this dog then.

A friend from Spain came to visit, he'd met Mini earlier and exclaimed what a lovely dog Mini Mouse was. I did mention at the time that Mini Mouse had a dark side but didn't have time to go into any detail. Enter my Spanish friend into my house for Sunday lunch. Announcing his presence with a bottle of wine in each hand and in the crucifix position. This level of joy was too much for Mini Mouse who thought it might be another kick in the head. He attacked immediately, the sight of a man dancing around my front room on one leg with two bottles of wine and a yorkie hanging off the end of his shoe was a sight to behold. They made friends eventually and settled down to a nice lunch. My Spanish friend fed the dog most of his dinner under the table to prevent another shoe attack.

Mini Mouse saw no profit in being friendly, he would attack anyone including the owner and myself if he had a suspicion that a kick in the head was forthcoming. One night in the gloom and bare footed I crossed my legs. Crossing your legs to a partially-sighted dog can appear as a failed attempt at a kick in the head. Latched on to my big toe with his one good tooth, Mini's body mass was dragging the tooth through the bottom of my toe like a razor blade. In defence I hit him on the nose (the only time I've hit a dog). Poor Mini Mouse hit the floor and jumped straight back up onto my lap, gave me a kiss and a look that said what just happened?

At first people thought I was a control freak as I constantly called to Mini Mouse on walks "here, here, here". This was of course so Mini Mouse would know where I was, it didn't mean come here. Later on when he was totally blind he would slide along the walls of the house until he found the kitchen door leading to the garden. Even in winter I kept the door open, it's better to be cold than suffer the puddles of pee brought on by Mini Mouse's diabetes. Not being a vet every tenth or twelfth time I injected Mini Mouse I would catch a nerve and he would squeal. He never went for me or prevented me from injecting him and always presented himself to me prostrate.

Sadly Mini Mouse died in my wife's arms in a vet's waiting room with me stroking his head. I phoned the owner who was in France to tell her the bad news. That was hard, I've never had a dog die on me before or since. I had to explain to the French owner that she had given me her live dog and I was arranging to have an urn with her dog's ashes sent to her. My brave little solider, Mini Mouse the fearless, I do miss him. Well apart from once when he was on a visit and greeted me in the usual way with lots of licks and kisses. The French owner in her sexy quaint accent said "Graham I must tell you this".

"What's that Lucie?", more licks and kisses from Mini.

"He eats shit", long pause as I gently but firmly pushed Mini Mouse away from my face saying "you could have mentioned that a bit earlier Lucie".

Foreign owners are not common with me and do have unexpected problems. Luna's owners were Polish and their dog was medium-sized and very good natured with an obsession with balls. They called her a red Labrador which I think was Polish for mongrel. The main problem with Luna was she wouldn't come back on walks when called. You couldn't properly exercise Luna on the lead but you couldn't trust her off the lead. When the owners returned I explained the predicament, the dog was out of control, she was disobedient and undisciplined. The owner promptly dropped a ball on the ground and told Luna to leave it which she did. He then told Luna to pick the ball up and put it into his hand which Luna did. The owner then said "how undisciplined is that?"

After some thought I said "yes but you're speaking in Polish". With that we all fell about laughing realizing the dog couldn't speak English.

The next time we had Luna I was unable to find *Polish for Beginners* in the library so I had to adapt. I found putting *ski* on the end of each word had the desired effect. So we had comeski, sitski, homeski etc. The unexpected part with Luna was she taught me Polish, after a fashion she seemed to understand if words sounded remotely east European and eventually became bilingual.

Luna had a curious effect on me by making me superstitious. It happened on New Year's morning whilst taking her for a walk. Picking up her toilet a turd made a bid for freedom by jumping out of the bag, like a fool and as a reflex action I caught it. I know what everyone is thinking but if I had made that one left-handed catch playing for England against Australia in an Ashes test match I'd have been given a knighthood! I dealt with the escapee and decided to wash my hands in the river whereupon I quickly slipped on the river bank and fell in the river. This remember all happened on New Year's morning leaving me to think a year's bad luck had all happened on one morning or it could be a very shitty year. The following week I bought a pair of dog-walking boots only to find back home I had two different sizes in the same box. Over the following month the broadband and telephone packed up three times followed by the hot water bottle leaking in the bed one night making me believe I had disgraced myself for the first time in sixty years. Needless to say I didn't buy a lottery ticket that month.

Maddie and Blaze are Manchester Terriers. The breed used to be called black and tan because of their colour. Their shape resembles a small Whippet but they also look like a small Doberman . In fact Dr. Doberman took Manchester Terriers and bred a giant strain of Manchester Terriers which he called Doberman. Although small, Manchester Terriers have a set of teeth and heart to match any Doberman. They live off their nerves and keep warm and alert by shivering, just in case a rat should chance walking across the front room floor.

Maddie and Blaze are mother and son. Angela was actually present when Blaze was conceived so we always felt a special kind of responsibility when they came to stay. Maddie would always clean her son's teeth and ears first thing in the morning even though he was much bigger than her. Blaze had a real set of nashers on him which he was always willing to display. This was especially so if he thought another dog or person was getting to close to his mum. At night both dogs had to be covered over by a blanket as if they were back in a cave.

The first time Blaze stayed he waited by the bed for the first snore and then got into bed, no, not on the bed, in the bed. He started at the foot of the bed and worked his way up. I awoke next morning at alarm call and thought I'd had a baby as Blaze was using my crotch as a pillow. Realizing I was awake Blaze crawled up to my face to give me a good morning kiss and thanked me for the night's warmth and shelter. Another time Angela had prepared me a beautiful ham-off-the-bone roll with seeds, pickle and everything. It was the best ham roll ever made, so I decided it deserved a glass of wine. Upon my return from the kitchen some twenty seconds later I found or rather didn't find the roll. Blaze had swallowed it whole, even worse Blaze jumped up onto my lap, kissed me and gave me that excited look of that was delicious can you get her to make another. I had my revenge on his subsequent visits by my making a point to eat a ham roll very slowly in front of him.

I have had somewhat similar experiences with other dogs. The three boys stayed once, two of them were as sweet as a nut the other one we nicknamed Billy the Kid. All three were rescue dogs but Billy the Kid was the one who was always in trouble. He threatened neighbours, went on walkabout and would even threaten the other two dogs at meal times. My Sunday dinner was sliced roast beef from Tesco's. The phone rang and after a brief time I returned to the kitchen, plastic bag but no roast beef. Now at my age I assumed the worst, I'd thrown the roast beef away and kept the plastic bag. I checked the bin but no roast beef. It suddenly occurred to me what might have happened, I turned to the three boys and said "who ate the roast beef", Billy the Kid dropped his head straight away.

Mystery solved and a cheese roll for Sunday lunch. I was unable to have the dogs again because of Billy the Kid's aggressive nature towards neighbours whose goodwill I needed, so Billy the Kid became unwanted.

Darcy was a nine-month-old Labrador, beautiful looking dog but young and foolish. I arrived home from the pub Saturday lunchtime. My wife greeted me by saying there's a problem. Now after being down the pub for two hours you don't really want to hear about a problem before you've taken your coat off. In a loud voice I enquired what the problem was, in a quiet voice Angela announced the dog has eaten Sunday dinner. Apparently my wife had purchased a beautiful spit-roasted chicken from our local butcher but had forgotten something and returned to the shop. On her return home five minutes later Darcy had managed to consume the whole chicken apart from two wings and half a leg left on the kitchen floor. I couldn't stop laughing edified by the thought that the chicken would have its revenge sometime later, it never did. The next day, Sunday Angela shot up to the supermarket to get another chicken. Re-entering the house Darcy was all nose in the air looking at my wife's shopping bag. He turned and looked at me but I already knew that he was thinking dinner going to be great today just like yesterday.

An even darker story revolves around Darcy the bear-like Labrador who had stayed many times. Darcy enjoyed his walks particularly lunchtime to the pub to meet his human friends. On a lunchtime visit two patrons came over to pet the dog. Having had a drink and being in high spirits they approached the tethered Darcy keen to pat his head without asking. Darcy wasn't enamoured by the men's behaviour or keen on letting them pat his head. The first chap being quick got away with it, the second bloke didn't and was gently nipped on the nose. As the man recoiled the gentle bite became a scratch and the man screamed for an ambulance to be called.

The speed at which an ambulance was called for seemed a bit odd at the time but I thought no more of it. A police investigation followed in accordance with pub health and safety rules and no further action was taken. A month later I received a letter from an ambulance-chasing solicitor requesting compensation for their client's scratched nose which may require plastic surgery!!

With legal advice I responded to the solicitor's letter outlining the facts and was subsequently threatened along with my whole family for the rest of our lives by the client (scratch nose). Being a pensioner and having a heart condition I thought scratch nose being at least half my age was trying with his threats to get a civic award for bravery, ho hum. The investigating officer at the time did intimate the police had been needlessly involved for compensation purposes. To date after two years and two different solicitor attempts nothing further has happened and I don't expect it to.

This experience left me wondering where common sense has gone, why are people so desperate and greedy and why the law doesn't automatically dissuade the senseless use of the law more often.

Max was a young (eight months) black Labrador, he had a head like a JCB bucket and a body to match. Now a local cat had the habit of coming around and sitting by next-door's fence preening itself. This I took as a deliberate act on the cat's part to tease and annoy my dogs. Max took the bait and barked. The cat carried on cleaning itself as usual safe in the knowledge that Max could do nothing because of the fence. Max started to cry in frustration, the smiling cat carried on teasing. Max could stand it no longer, I watched in horror as he backed up and galloped towards the fence. It was like watching a cartoon, Max hit the fence and went through it like a bulldozer. The hole left had the shape of his body. The cat although stunned managed to escape up a tree. We never did see that cat again and thereafter always referred to Max as Mad Max.

I take Mad Max down the pub every day. I don't like it but he does, all the attention and a chance of a scrap or two. I always tell people the problem, if Max feels he's not had enough tickle tums he gives out a very loud bark. It's not aggression it's that he simply feels he deserves more. One day when it was cold and wet I decided it would be too uncomfortable for Max and left him at home. Did he get the hump or what. When I returned home he picked up his lead and thrust it into my hand. Feeling suitably guilty I went straight back out with him in the pouring rain. Not an ideal situation for me having just returned from the pub but the woods were very quiet just like a male urinal.

Some of my rescue dogs come with serious problems from their past. Not their fault you just have to carry on and cope. Rocco had been rescued from Battersea Dogs Home. His owner was a musician who worked nights. Sadly Rocco's owner fell ill and had to stay long term in hospital. He passed Rocco onto his son who was also a musician who worked nights. The son eventually realised he couldn't cope and returned Rocco back to Battersea Dogs Home. On hearing this the father discharged himself from hospital and rescued Rocco once again. The owner had heard of me and brought Rocco to me for what could have been a year's stay and then went straight back to hospital.

I knew Rocco would be a problem having been in and out and around-about dog kennels. So it proved. After the owner left Rocco flew under the kitchen table and could not be moved. I knew what was afoot and sure enough Rocco pissed and messed on the kitchen floor. I just cleared up the mess and the dog watched me from a safe distance. He seemed staggered by the fact I hadn't inflicted pain or punishment upon him. Sure enough in the dark (10 pm) and after eighteen hours Rocco decided to test my trustworthiness. He came from under the kitchen table into the front room and bumped his head on my knee. I in part ignored him and carried on watching t.v. A little later on I tickled him behind the ear and Rocco suddenly became my dog. He jumped up onto my lap and demanded lots of stroking to make up for the past eighteen hours. The dog never left my side again. The owner returned after only a few weeks his illness not being as bad as first thought. He was pleased to see Rocco run straight to me along the settee back and place himself around my neck and shoulders for protection.

Having a wicked sense of humour can sometimes be embarrassing. Spritzer is a mongrel but has a beautiful dappled black and white coat and the shape of a basset hound. The dog had the rare ability to be able to submerge underwater, eyes open head and nose fully under. A chap passing by the river exclaimed "that's most unusual what breed is she".

As a joke I replied "its a Norwegian Spritzer, they use them in Norway to catch salmon". The man who was looking to buy an unusual dog joined me and started to ask me all sorts of questions regarding pedigree and breeders. Being embarrassed for the man and indeed myself I kept up the pretence. I do hope the man didn't spend too long a time finding out there's no such breed as the Norwegian Spritzer, or perhaps there is. The dog must have developed his underwater swimming for a reason surely!

Spritzer's owner worked for the police and therefore had irregular patterns of activity. Dogs as pets do like a plan they can follow. Spritzer was no different as she patiently watched me shave, get dressed and drink tea. She wasn't so much interested in these rituals but in noticing how much closer she was to her morning walk and swim. By the time I reached the walk ritual: hat, coat, shoes, keys, mess bags and lead Spritzer would be crying with excitement. This was in direct contrast to her owners usual day which could be a bit erratic. Subsequently when the owner arrived to collect Spritzer she hid. The owner suggested Spritzer hadn't yet realized who she was. In truth Spritzer had indeed realised who she was and was trying to vote with her feet.

It's always somewhat difficult when dogs are trying to demonstrate they'd rather not go home. Lotte was a ten-month-old Golden Retriever who really loved her walks and playing with other dogs. When it came to leaving time I walked her across the road to her owner's car. I kissed Lotte and told her to be good. Upon reaching the front garden path I looked back to wave Lotte off. Lotte had a look that she had just realized what was happening. She looked at the boot of the car and then at me. Suddenly Lotte laid down and rolled on her back refusing to get into the car boot. I had to go and sit on the back seat of the owner's car before Lotte would jump into the boot of the car. The second time Lotte had to leave she wouldn't fall for the back seat trick again. This second time I had to climb into the boot before she would get in, I escaped over the back seat and out the door otherwise she would have made me go home with her, a new variation on dog-napping.

It's not only the dogs which have unusual characters, sometimes the owners can appear a bit odd. A girl phoned to ask if I would look after her Standard Poodle for the weekend as she was going racing in her MGB. Nothing really untoward there then. When the girl turned up she was eight months pregnant, I didn't think an eight month pregnant girl could fit behind the wheel of an MGB but she can, apparently. It got worse, what she had failed to mention was the Standard Poodle was bright pink with a standard lion cut!

Fearing for my image I took the dog out at dusk and dawn but of course managed to bump into everyone I knew. It gets worse the dog liked to roam in the woods and I kept in contact by frequently calling her back to me, her name was Precious. People thought I had changed my nature as I called out Precious come here and the pink poodle turned up.

I took Precious to the local pub with trepidation as it is frequented by hard men. I had no reason to worry as to a man they fell in love with Precious. They made such a fuss of her, she loved it and I felt guilty about having tried to hide her under the table. Sometime later Precious's owner bought another dog to keep Precious company. It was the biggest great Dane I've ever seen, what did she call him? Dave. Perhaps he reminded her of a previous boyfriend, he was a very big boy. Was the girl owner eccentric or what!

On occasions you drop yourself in it without realizing because of dogs. A young attractive woman used to walk her Golden Retriever through the woods. Her dog who I never looked after would always approach me and lie on her back to have her tummy tickled. One day whilst talking to a group of dog walkers over came the Retriever for her tickle. Without thinking and out loud I said "here comes the tart". A man in the group said "thanks for the tip" and walked away before I could explain it was the dog I was referring to and not the owner. I never did see that girl in the woods again.

Another time I put my foot in it I was talking to another gaggle of dog walkers. One dog suddenly mounted another with an obvious urgency. To make light of the situation I said I wished all dog walkers would greet one another in a similar fashion, (the gaggle were all female except me). Then one of the gaggle pointed out that both dogs were male. "Forget everything I've just said" I said and embarrassedly walked away.

Do wild animals take drugs or just know you're harmless? Squirrels do. I believe squirrels can work out whether a dog is on the lead or its fitness and adjust their alarm/runaway time accordingly. One day whilst walking a dog through the woods with my wife a squirrel jumped from a tree onto my shoulder. The squirrel either as high as a kite or retarded then begun to preen itself. Having attended to his ablutions whilst I was still walking he clambered down my torso and squirrelled his way back into the undergrowth. I turned to my wife and enquired if she knew what this meant, "no". I've lost all my masculine powers, even wild animals are not afraid of me any more! The dog I was walking at the time just stood there looking at me. He couldn't believe it either.

I strongly believe dogs can tell much more than we think through their noses. A Fox Terrier visited and took particular interest in our 200-foot garden spending hours sniffing every inch. Later, on his first night he woke us by barking. We, thinking the Fox Terrier needed the toilet, let him out the back door whereupon he flew down the garden. This carried on for a further five times that night and every night he stayed. I worked out the Fox Terrier could tell the time within minutes of when the numerous foxes in our area crossed the garden. At the allotted time without fail he would bark to go out and try to ambush a fox. It was worse than having a baby in the house, we finished up by taking it in turns to let the dog out to cut down on our sleep deprivation.

Dogs like humans can suffer mental-health problems. Daisy was a young Basset Hound (ears touching the ground), she thought she was pregnant. In order to make a nest she dug out the carpet in all four corners of every room she could get into. Her big bloodshot eyes were as excellent at sight as her big paws were at digging. She would bury part of her food in the garden for the coming pups. Should Daisy catch sight of anyone watching her she would wait and dig the food up and rebury it somewhere else fearing theft from her pups.

Her phantom pregnancy culminated in a secure pub garden. She explored as usual every corner of the garden for suitable nest sites. The garden being fenced all round gave me a false sense of security and, unconcerned about Daisy's antics, I read the newspaper. After half an hour I thought I best check up on Daisy and see what nest site she had chosen. Couldn't find her, and to add to the panic my wife entered the pub. She said "where's the dog"? I replied "I CANT FIND THE DOG". Two bags of shopping jumped out of her hands (box of eggs included) as she placed her hands on her head and screamed "YOUV'E LOST THE DOG". I in a similar fashion with hands on my head screamed back "I'VE LOST THE DOG". It was at this moment the pub chief emerged with Daisy over his shoulder enquiring if the dog was ours. Apparently Daisy smelling the food had decided that the pub kitchen would make an excellent nest site and promptly dug a hole under the fence and was preparing a nest site in the corner of the pub kitchen.

Sadly the pub staff took a fancy to Daisy and didn't bar her. This gave rise to another escape problem. Daisy had decided that the pub was no longer a suitable nest site due to disturbance issues. On her next visit therefore she planned her escape. Sure enough as soon as someone with a pint in each hand pushed open the garden door she was straight through his legs into the main bar and out the back-door and into a busy street. Daisy's short crocodilian legs were propelling her up the central white line at such a speed her ears had taken off from the ground and were flapping by the side of her head like wings.

With half the pub in hot pursuit and to their credit all traffic at a standstill we finally caught up with Daisy in somebody's front garden. She was surveying it as you might have guessed as being a suitable site for the phantom pups.

What a cow Daisy was on her morning walks. If she thought she wanted or needed a longer walk or hadn't met enough new friends she would defiantly cross the river and stubbornly refuse to come back to my call. This led to a number of local dog walkers believing "DAISY YOU COW GET BACK HERE", was in fact her registered kennel club name.

We didn't see Daisy for eighteen months, she spotted us some distance away in the woods (excellent eye sight remember). She greeted and kissed us and we in turn patted and affectionately called her Daisy the cow. The owner's father turned up and announced he now looked after Daisy when the owners were on holiday. I suspect that was because Daisy had grown out of digging up carpets to make nests. We eventually parted and Daisy followed us, the owner's father called out don't worry she always does this, you carry on, she'll come back to me. He kept calling to Daisy and she did stop. We were two hundred metres apart with Daisy in the middle. She looked a bit fraught, she looked at the owner's father who was by now constantly calling her and then she looked at us as we moved further away. Suddenly Daisy made a decision and scampered up to us. The owner's father as a face-saving exercise caught us up and joined us on our walk. We all knew given the choice Daisy would have rather come home with us than the father. What a cow Daisy is!

I once or twice had the good fortune to dog walk overseas. I would visit a good friend of mine in Spain who had three rescue dogs Luna, Tuppence Half Penny and Sprat. Tuppence Half Penny was rescued from an airport and had the wanderlust. She disappeared for eighteen months once and then turned up as if she'd just been out for a pint of milk. She must have had aboriginal blood as she was always going on walkabout. The three dogs were dearly loved by my friend and his garden was a good safe place to be. Unfortunately my friend was away on business many times a year so the dogs didn't have as many walks as both parties would have wished for.

When I stayed with my friend Luna a big Labrador used to sleep on the bed with us in order to know when we would wake to take him out for a walk. We tried kicking him off the bed but he was just too big and heavy. Besides his enthusiasm at seeing his walk buddies made you feel somewhat special. Our walks would last about two hours through the Spanish wooded hillsides. The walks were lovely except for the beginning and end. Let me explain that many dogs in Spain are kept for security reasons not primarily as pets. Most dogs are confined to their gardens and not taken for walks. The three musketeers (Luna, Tuppence Half Penny and Sprat) were exceptions as my friend's house had been burgled several times. On one occasion the burglars had tied the dogs to the outside fence so they wouldn't wander off. Viscious guard dogs they were not.

When I took the three musketeers for a walk they would run the wrong way down the village street. Tuppence Half Penny first followed by Sprat and finally lumbering Luna. They would raise the alarm call with the guard dogs at the first house and then proceed up the street raising the alarm house by house. The three musketeers would let every guard dog in the village know they were going for a walk. As we left the village for our country walk you could hear for miles around dogs crying, howling and barking. When we returned to the village some two hours later the three musketeers would announce their return to the village guard dogs and declare what a lovely time they had had. The cacophony of sound would begin all over again.

Tuppence Half Penny as mentioned was an airport rescue very people friendly but was also an opportunist when it came to scraps of food. He was the first one to be poisoned and died in agony as no vet was available due to a festival. Sprat was poisoned a short while later. Whether it was an accident with rat poison or a deliberate act by a villager with over-sensitive ears we'll never know. Luna died a few years later of old age, thank god. I still miss the three musketeers on my Spanish visits.

Shih Tzu, being oriental dogs, can be very proud as mentioned before. They are the quintessential lap dog. The name I was told means lion face in Chinese but I prefer the other definition as a zoo that has no animals. Ronnie and Reggie were brothers, we called them the Krays. They liked watching rugby with me, one under each arm sitting on their back legs, looking somewhat like pandas. Ronnie and Reggie were never seen more than few yards from each other. Reggie had an under shot jaw and slept with part of his tongue sticking out of his mouth as if dead. Although small Shih Tzu have a long back in proportion to their size. Consequently they had a long and expensive history with the vet. This was due to their habit of play fighting first thing in the morning and jumping around on the furniture like squirrels.

On one stay with us Reggie went crook, he didn't get out of the bed he shared with Ronnie. Ronnie was distraught as Reggie refused to play fight or move. Having not drunk or eaten, or moved out of his bed for two days my nerve broke. I phoned the vet who confirmed registration and insurance. With no hesitation I took Reggie up to the vet (Sunday morning) bed and all. I placed the bed on the vet's table and she examined poor Reggie's back. Finding nothing untoward she stated she would have to run a few tests. "A few tests" I said (in an emotional voice) he's insured do every test you've got, just give me back my dog fit and well. The open cheque I just written brought glee to the vet's face Reggie on the other hand having just had a thermometer removed from his backside looked less than pleased.

Ronnie had a terrible time with his brother away overnight, he couldn't rest in his bed all alone. Next day I returned to the vet who explained it was probably a gut infection and after treatment the dog would be fine and able to go home. The vet went to take Reggie's temperature and upon seeing the thermometer Reggie sat down and refused to stand for rectal insertion. That's when I knew Reggie could never be gay. Ronnie was particularly pleased to see his brother return home. Unfortunately the owners upon return from their expensive holiday were less than pleased to find a vet bill for hundreds of pounds. They phoned the vet for a meeting to discuss why they had been paying out for Reggie's back treatment when it was a gut problem all along. Even worse because of the medical history the insurance premium had become too great and they were no longer insured. The owner did thank me for my prompt action and explained the insurance had gone sky high because Ronnie and Reggie's allergy to offal which is often in dog food. Two things now sprang to mind, the first was in good faith I'd spent the uninsured owner's money as if it were water. The second was I recalled the day before Reggie went tom and dick my wife and I had had liver and bacon for dinner. Surely to god Reggie hadn't jumped into the bin eaten the leftovers and jumped back out again. Impossible I thought but then remember the Krays ability to transform into squirrels. Being a coward I said nothing but my wife and I never had liver and bacon (one of my favourites) when the Krays came to stay.

Not all of my visitors have been as welcome as most. Paddy for instance was a black Cocker Spaniel who was as mad as a hatter, no I mean really mad. Paddy had attacked the owners several times for no apparent reason. Even more worrying he had attacked their grandchildren whose parents now understandably refused to visit.

The husband was all for having Paddy put down but his wife was far from keen. This led to conflict in the couple's fifty-year-old marriage. I interceded and offered for free to take Paddy for a week to see what could be done. Paddy was a normal dog at first but as time went by and his confidence grew his true character came out. Paddy would show affection and in the next instance display aggression. He would muzzel you to have a stroke or tickle and then in the blink of an eye try to sever your hand from your wrist.

The second night of Paddy's stay he went to bed by the side of my wife who had retired early. Two hours later I retired only to find upon entry to the bedroom my way blocked by Paddy's manic eyes and pure white teeth. Keeping me out of the comforts of the marital bed was for me grounds for a lethal injection. The following night I had a plan to avoid the spare bedroom. My wife went to bed and I kept Paddy downstairs with me so he wouldn't feel the need to be on guard. Eventually Paddy and I headed for the sack. Upon reaching the wooden ladder to the land of nod Paddy shot past me to the top of the stairs where he stood on viscious guard. Not being able to reach the spare bedroom and having to spend the night on the settee I thought was worthy of two lethal injections.

The owners of Paddy duly turned up at the end of the week and asked how things had gone. "Put your dog down" I said "we've done our best and there is no hope". Sadly it took another year before the wife upon returning from hospital with facial stitches finally bit the bullet and said Paddy's got to go. Sad yes but children and people's safety should come first. Like people some dogs can be a menace and are best kept out of the gene pool.

Bentley was a Labradoodle whose breed has several permutations being a cross between a Labrador and a poodle. Bentley at ten months old had reached the size of a short Irish Wolfhound. The owner's father had declined holiday care after Bentley had chewed the steering wheel off his car whilst he'd stopped for a newspaper. Bentley's erratic behaviour now became our problem. Being a pup Bentley was into mouthing and upon his first visit he gave us a demonstration. Bentley mouthed my wife's hand to the extent it became painful and she screamed. Bentley took the scream as enjoyment and therefore bit harder. I had to physically manhandle Bentley off my wife and into the garden. I left Bentley in the garden for some time whilst I attended to my wife, giving him time to calm down. To this day if I say to Bentley "garden" he runs upstairs in the belief his done something wrong and the garden is a form of punishment.

To make matters worse the owners thought Bentley (having failed boot camp) would moderate his behaviour if he had a brother. They bought another Labradoodle this time in brown. Bentley of course became more competitive and naughtier in a quest for more attention. Rocco (the brown one) had a different temperament altogether and could be trusted off the lead. Whist walking Bentley one day another dog also called Bentley (a Boxer, also one of mine) responded to my constant calls of Bentley get here. The trouble was there was a road in between me and Bentley the Boxer. Instinctively

I jumped into the middle of the road to prevent him being run over as he raced to greet me. This is a good example of how man or beast can be hurt in a traffic accident just because of mistaken identity.

Bentley being naturally mischievous was always getting poor Rocco into trouble. I went shopping, well the wife shops and I patiently wait in the pub, used more or less as a pack horse. Upon our return home the front room floor was covered in cushion filler, it resembled two inches of snow. In a stern voice I cried out "who's done this". Poor Rocco, fearing a smack, wet himself straight away all over the kitchen floor. Poor Rocco it seemed was used to being punished as well for Bentley's vandalism.

My wife was never keen on black Bentley due to the chewing of the wrist incident. The cushion filler incident didn't help nor the constant bullying of brown Rocco. Imagine her horror then upon bringing me an early morning cup of tea in bed to find Bentley in bed with me. Stretched full out under the duvet with his head on the pillow. To make matters worse in my sleep I'd turned over and had Bentley in a half embrace. My wife seeing my arm around Bentley's torso cried out with a hint of jealousy "what's going on here". I just awaking and hearing her voice thought this woman imac hair treatment isn't working. Fortunately we both came round to seeing the funny side of the situation.

Flo, Hattie, Troy and Owen were owned by a very nice couple who seemed to specialize in rescuing Border Collies, all except Owen who was a retired guide dog for the blind. Flo had the distinction of being the only dog I've ever walked in the street without a lead. She never faltered, left or right, never distracted. Hattie was probably the cleverest dog I've ever come across and I've had quite a few Border Collies! Hattie taught me a game where I had to take on the posture of a giant squirrel and chase her down the garden as she whined and cried in pretend fear. The end game being she would make a bolt to escape past me without my laying a finger on her. Once past me the game would start all over again and continue on and off all day. I thought this was a game played with the owners but it turned out they had no idea of the game and it was taught only to me. This made me feel somewhat privileged.

Having an intelligent dog like Hattie over a period of time leads you to be in tune with each other to the extent you can understand what's being said without the use of language. One day Hattie went to the back door, her speak for I want to go to the toilet or ambush something. Instead of racing down the garden to play the giant squirrel game or ambush a cat she just stood there. Puzzled I looked down the garden and realized it was raining. I foolishly said to Hattie its raining, Hattie then looked up, I looked up to see all the washing on the line. Before I could look back down and announce I'd better get the washing in

Hattie was already walking back to the front room. She had a look on her face signalling how stupid she thought I was.

Troy replaced Flo when she died, poor Troy had had a terrible time of it when she was a pup. Rescued I believe from north Wales where sheep dogs aren't worth a light unless working. Troy's brothers and sisters were probably drowned at birth as not being worth feeding. The only thing that saved Troy was being born with a silver coat, hence the name Troy after the weight measure for silver. Troy's unusual coat had the prospect of being worth something and so she was kept alive but not socialized. Consequently Troy stayed clear of other dogs and would not allow anyone to touch her unless she knew and trusted them.

My wife and I were constantly warning people not to touch the dog as a pat on the head could result in the loss of a finger. Troy probably picked up this anti-social behaviour as a pup. This was possibly the result of being picked up by the neck and thrown; not really her fault then. Although Troy had problems we did all the normal things, down the pub, walks etc. but always gave the warning "don't touch the dog".

Sitting in a pub garden one day a drunken man approached Troy who was on the lead. The usual warning was given but the drunk just said "no, all dogs love me". Its surprising how quick a drunk's reflexes can be as he recoiled back and saved at least one finger. The man's wife was none too pleased until I mentioned a warning had been given but not adhered to. I then went on to outline Troy's life experiences to date, including being chained up in an M.F.I. wardrobe for a year covered in her own mess. At the end of my explanation of Troy's behaviour the couple were almost in tears threatening to buy me and my wife a pint and Troy a steak.

The message in this story is always ask the owner before touching a dog and listen to what they say. It's no good seeing the owner receiving kisses or stroking and patting his dog and think its safe I'll be okay.

When Hattie died along came Owen, a retired guide dog for the blind and did Owen enjoy his retirement and being out of harness. The tragedy here is Owen tried to keep up with Troy in a race to ambush a garden crosser. Owen's back legs had gone early with the traditional problem of hip displacement, hence his early retirement. Poor Owen after his ambush exertions had to be lifted by the back legs and wheelbarrowed into the house. Whether a dog lover or not if years of Owen's loyal service to the blind, and early departure from life doesn't move you nothing will and you shouldn't read any further as you'd be beyond human help.

Holly was another Golden Retriever, young but with all those children in the house grossly overweight. All those treats and tit bits were not going to see her make old bones. Sure enough on a trip to the vets this prophecy was explained to the owners. The owners then went the other way and put Holly on a strict diet. Holly started to waste away. This all culminated in the night before she was due to stay with me. In her hunger she managed to climb onto the owners' dining table and proceeded to eat all the travelers cheques and dollars destined to be spent at Disney World Florida. I ensured Holly was stuffed during her stay with me, well I didn't want her to eat my money. I also watched her carefully at toilet times just in case the saying was true, where there's muck there's brass. I suspect that upon the owners return Holly was put upon a more money-friendly diet.

Maisy first stayed when she was young, recovering from major re-constructive surgery to her leg after a road accident. Being a young and foolish Springer Spaniel she would always rise to the challenge of beating you to the top of the stairs. Having half a scaffold pole pinned to the outside of her leg Maisy managed to take off large chunks of wallpaper along the entire length of the staircase. Apart from this irritating staircase-race habit Maisy, being a rescue dog, had a neglect problem. If you talked to someone or weren't paying her the required amount of attention to Maisy she would become very mischievous to gain the high ground attention wise. Her favourite trick was to steal items she thought would be precious. She would watch and note the portable items you used most. Hence the t.v. gun, glasses, pipe, lighter and in fact anything touched on a regular basis was paraded around the house to get attention or be chased. To this day I still have a glasses case, pipe and lighter with her teeth marks customizing my property should I be burgled.

The last time Maisy came she was recovering from an operation after swallowing a needle. We thought she had grown out of the stealing habit and therefore relaxed our guard. Maisy had in fact stopped parading stolen goods but the stealing carried on in secret. Maisy had changed tack to stealing what she thought you wouldn't miss so glasses case and t.v. gun were okay. Being a pipe smoker I have a large number of lighters on the mantlepiece, just in case. After about a week I noticed I was hunting around more and more for a light. Maisy was under suspicion but nothing could be proved and Maisy had the look of you never saw me so it was not me. I did find one lighter under the armchair, the other six or seven will probably turn up when they jam the lawnmower!

The Rough Collie (lassie type) Sable is a tragic tale and one I have very strong mixed feelings about. Sometimes you do what appears to be the right thing and it evolves into something else. Sable was rescued from her "gipsy" owners having been short chained for most of her young life. Consequently she had trouble walking and her teeth were mangled as a result of trying to chew through her chains. A lady realised the dog's plight and bought or should it be paid a ransom for the dog's freedom. The lady however found she couldn't cope with all Sable's problems and Sable found her way to a very poorly-sighted woman who was unable to take Sable for walks. This was where my wife and I came in but sadly because of the chaining and rarely being walked Sable could only manage a hundred yards in twenty minutes.

My wife phoned me in tears having turned up at the blind lady's house to take Sable for her walk, there was terrible trouble at the owner's house. I rushed around to find Sable had messed in the house and the owner being blind had been treading the mess all over her front room. Even worse the owner was on the phone to Battersea Dogs Home requesting they collect the dog as she couldn't cope. The owner became angry when Battersea informed her they didn't collect and the dog must be delivered to them. In a very distressed state the owner threatened to have the dog put down. Hearing this I went into crisis mode and offered to take the dog and find it a home or take it to a specialist rescue centre. The owner agreed and signed the dog over to me and we left for home with all Sable's toys and bedding.

I then went on a quest to find a suitable new owner, not an easy task with Sable's medical problems. Word got back to the previous owner that I was touting her dog about which in a sense was true. The blind lady phoned me and asked me directly how much I was asking for her dog; I assured her I wasn't looking for reward. Having already found a suitable new owner I gave her their phone number and she duly phoned them to see if I was lying, nice eh!

The new owners were a youngish professional couple who had the money to sort out Sable's teeth. They also had the energy and patience to get Sable back on her feet. In fact after a while they managed to get Sable fit enough to go jogging with them whereas before walking had been difficult for Sable. The new owners were into fitness, healthy living and sports. The husband was in training for a triathlon and whilst out training one day dropped dead with a heart attack. His wife in shock, distraught and slightly off the rails then made, in my opinion a big mistake. She had Sable put down a couple of weeks after her husband's funeral citing Sable's back leg problems. I know of two households in my street who would have taken Sable in, one being me and the other the husband's ex-wife.

Within two years of being rescued from the so called gipsies Sable was dead. Everybody involved in the chain of rescue had passed the dog onto a worse fate even though they had the best of intentions. Every time I think of Sable I feel guilty about my role in that chain. I wish emotionally I hadn't become involved but of course it was emotion that compelled me to become involved in the first place.

Sometimes you can form a relationship with dogs for no apparent reason. Millie is a small hairy Jack Russell whose lady owner we would regularly greet whilst dog walking. Little Millie loved chasing other dogs and scampering in and out of the river. Being the owners first dog she treated Millie as one of her own children. Imagine then the horror when you can see a life-threatening situation but are powerless to act as a loved one faces certain death.

What had happened was after several days of heavy rain the river had become swollen and was in full spate. Bold but foolish little Millie failed to understand the environmental facts. Millie jumped into the river as part of her usual chase, escape ploy and morning bath. The lady owner froze to the spot with fear. I passed our dog lead to my wife and ran downriver in the hope of intercepting Millie who was by now being tossed and turned in the river current. Downstream I had a few moments to think. Would I be able to keep my balance in wellingtons against the force of the river? Would I be able to snatch Millie as she went by, as there would be only one chance to save her?

The situation resolved itself as Millie being swept around a bend managed to climb out on the opposite bank and went to ground knowing now something awful was about to happen. The owner's daughter ran around over the nearest bridge and brought Millie back. Having dry feet I joined the the group where Millie's owner was clutching Millie to her ample bosom. Seeing the owner was still in a state of shock I tried to lighten the moment by commenting that I bet she could really want to hurt Millie at that moment, (I knew she never would). Upon hearing this the owner clutched Millie even tighter to her bosom. I had to walk on because I had the urge to stroke Millie but felt it might all go terribly wrong.

Millie after the river incident always greeted me whereas before she would ignore me and just play with other dogs. Did she have a sixth sense or what? The other odd thing was I bumped into the owner sometime later in a local supermarket and suggested she may want to get her husband interested in the half price boxes of chocolates on offer as I was doing for my wife. If looks could kill, I only found out later that she was going through a divorce process and my comments had been taken the wrong way. Regardless of this Millie still rushes over to me on walks and paws my knee before turning over to have her stomach tickled.

I've had other experiences of dogs who don't know me showing trust and affection but how would my wife and I have a reputation reaching the island of Kos? Not being solely beach people we caught a bus into Kos town. As we boarded the crowded bus an Alsatian dog got on at the middle exit door and proceeded along the bus to where my wife and I were standing. Standing passengers were cautiously moving out of the Alsatian's way until the dog reached me and my wife whereupon he laid down across our feet pinning us to the floor. Being an observant kind of chap I had noticed the large sign above the bus driver's head indicating no dogs were allowed on the bus. I gently tapped the bus driver's shoulder and pointed to the dog on my feet. The laid-back driver just shrugged his shoulders and drove off. Don't you just love the Greeks.

After about seven miles the totally relaxed Alsatian got up and released our pins-and-needle feet from his weight. The Alsatian then walked to the driver's door whereupon the driver pulled over and the dog got off (he must have been on a hot date). My wife said the dog was extremely clever to be able to catch a bus and know where to get off. My reply was the dog is stupid he got on at the exit door and got off at the entrance door. By the time we and half the bus had stopped laughing the blood had returned back to our feet.

Dolly was a lovely black Labrador whose principle owner doted on. Having met the owner on dog walks he felt confident Dolly would be well looked after. With confidence tinged with a little apprehension he brought Dolly and left for his holiday. The owner only phoned once or twice whilst on holiday and was assured Dolly had taken to us like a duck to water. Nevertheless I received a late night call from the owner (late night calls are normally grief). Dolly's owner explained he was walking along the runway to catch his flight home and could he pick Dolly up when he landed around 2 am that morning. Realizing the man's love and want for his dog I of course agreed. At about 3 am he turned up with his daughter to collect Dolly. Although staying close by me Dolly became very excited when the owner's daughter produced a lead.

Dolly always liked going out whatever the weather or time of day. The sight of the lead would always drive her crazy and once on the lead she would pull to the front door as if possessed. I suddenly called out to Dolly as she pawed the front door "is that it then, no kiss". Dolly immediately and just as unexpectedly turned round jumped up on the chair and kissed me. The large man of an owner observing this welled up and put his hand to his heart. Choking back the tears he said goodnight and left realizing he'd seen a side to his dog he never knew existed and that he was not now the only man in Dolly's life. The next time I heard from Dolly's owner he phoned to say he'd just been invited to a family wedding in Canada. He went on to say he wouldn't be going to Canada unless I could look after Dolly. No pressure there then but fortunately I could have Dolly. She still greets and says goodbye with a kiss every time I encounter her.

Lulu was a similar story, being a very young Cocker Spaniel she was into everything. Lulu's owner was a big man-of-the-world taxi driver who had never had children or a dog before. He once took Lulu to the vets declaring she must be unwell because she spends all day sniffing the garden and woods. The vets reply was the obvious she's a Cocker Spaniel!

Recommended by Dolly's owner the big taxi driver booked Lulu in with us for two weeks. Lulu and the owner duly turned up. Lulu being young and inquisitive was all over the house and garden in five minutes. If gifted with speech she would have been able to advise on every event or visitor over the last five years whether they be human or animal (what a nose). Now we come to the tragic bit. My wife said what a beautiful dog and enquired how old Lulu was. The macho taxi driver now sobbed as he blurted out Lulu was only six months old and never been left alone (the two week holiday looked in doubt). The owner eventually pulled himself together and apologized to my wife saying you must think I'm a right wally. Gathering himself together Lulu's owner left but phoned every day from Turkey to check on Lulu. Each time the owner phoned he said sorry he wouldn't be phoning again, but of course he did.

I had an indication of Lulu's owner's feelings about his dog on a dog walk with him. He told me a Rottweiler had threatened Lulu on her walk a few days before. He informed the Rottweiler's owner that if ever his dog hurt Lulu he would kill him and his dog. Needless to say no one has seen the Rottweiler or owner since. Thank god Lulu always greets my wife and me with a kiss, think how it might be if she showed fear towards us. My wife's name is used as an enticement to get Lulu back into the house from the garden. The thought my wife may be at the front door appears to be the only thing to override Lulu's sniffing quest.

Teddy is a Swedish Vallhund, used in Sweden for rounding up cattle. A lovely natured dog which resembles a very large corgi or even better a small Alsatian with its legs sawn off half way up. If I was in a room you can be sure little Ted was also there, if I went out little Ted went with me. Ted was simply a dog you couldn't resist. Being of high latitude origin Ted's main interest in life was food, in human terms he wasn't so much a connoisseur more a consumer. Any food with not too many vegetables would do and consequently he was on siege-type rations. On one pub visit he managed to acquire spare rib bones and the same night sicked up a bleached bone in every room in the house.

On one of Ted's frequent visits he woke me at 4.30 am. Fearing he needed the toilet I let him into the garden. No it wasn't the garden he wanted as he stared at his lead making the most pitiful sound you can imagine. So out on a walk we went, it's hard to resist little Ted. Ted's owner was obviously an early riser and as we reached the woods at 5 am I was surprised to see how many men were walking their dogs before going to work. Little Ted ran over to a large number of these men and received a treat. I'd heard of drugs dogs but a treat dog, never. Ted had the ability to know if a stranger had treats on them and would sit at their feet until he received a treat, irresistible.

The other unusual thing about Ted was rain, he just doesn't like it. I went to Sweden once and it rained every day. With a Swedish ancestry and originally being used to rounding up cattle all day you'd think Ted would have a better understanding of the environment, but no. He wouldn't even go into the garden for a toilet if it was raining. On walks if we were caught in a shower he would shelter under a dry spot from over hanging trees and look as if he'd stay put for a month if necessary until the rain had passed. Most peculiar.

Molly the Tibetan Terrier was misnamed she should have been called Houdini. The first day Molly stayed I saw another Tibetan terrier walking up the street on its own. Typical I thought, never seen the breed before and then you see another one straight away. The terrier walking up the street was the spitting image of Molly. A micro-second later I realized it was Molly she'd jumped out the window. Fifteen minutes later with half the street forming a road block we ended Molly's bid for freedom.

A few days later my son offered to take Molly for a walk after school, which was nice. This resulted in major roads being blocked temporarily as my son and his classmates chased after Molly who had somehow slipped her collar. The posse finally cornered Molly in an underpass three quarters of a mile from the house. The end result was my son vowed he would never walk another dog as it was too stressful. Still his good intentions were well meant for the little time they lasted.

At the end of Molly's stay she escaped again from the back garden at day break. Sunday mornings are quiet but I still expected to find Mollie dead by the kerb side as I frantically searched for two hours in the car. Distraught I returned home and my wife thought she had good news, Molly had been found. Dismay now turned to anger and revenge, "I'll bounce that dog off all four walls" I said and my wife half believed me. My wife insisted on accompanying me to prevent Molly being bounced off all four walls. And so we set off, I don't really know what Tibetan terriers eat in Tibet but I suspect it's scraps and bones. Molly was found in a graveyard, sitting on a grave looking down at the ground. When I turned up at the graveyard office the lady in charge said Molly had sore paws. Upon hearing Molly had a slight injury I left the office in case I broke down. With head in hands revenge had very quickly turned to relief and remorse. After arriving home I returned to the graveyard office with a box of chocolates for the graveyard lady but I was unable to speak to her as I passed over the chocolates. Houdini (Molly) was given safely back to the owners without any mention of the chaos the escape artist had caused.

I've observed in human life hen-pecked husbands, sad but you mustn't interfere, but when it's dogs who are hen-pecked it seems more tragic. Two staffs came to stay. The male was big the wife (what a bitch) was half his size but wasn't dominated in any way by her husband. The poor husband would try and get peace by sitting next to me. If this was spotted the wife would immediately jump onto the settee and force the husband off. If I played tug-of-war with the husband she would immediately jump in (watch your fingers time) and snatch my end. The growling and swearing over the tug-of-war rope became so bad that neighbours thought I was holding dog fights in the back yard. It didn't seem to matter how aggressive the wife became the husband always deferred.

I've had other dog husbands suffering at the hands of their wives. Three Jack Russells paid a visit, two bitches and a dog. The dog was as nice as nice could be, he had to be as the two bitches would constantly bicker and worse. The husband would jump up onto my lap when the wives kicked off. We would watch together as the wives fought over toys, beds and who had just kissed the husband. You would have thought long ago they would have sorted out who was number one and number two wife, but no. The husband had become oblivious to the girls' antics and would often go to sleep during a ruck.

The funniest thing I ever witnessed was after their dinner time. Each dog had its own coloured bowl and a truce always prevailed whilst feeding. Ten minutes after a feed in the garden I was washing up (rare for me) and witnessed one of the bitches go out into the garden and urinate in the other bitch's food bowl. I thought it was an accident until five minutes later the other bitch came out and urinated into the other bitch's food bowl. Happy families eh!

Ollie and Jake were Hungarian Vizslas whom we always had to stay over Christmas and New Year. Jake was a lovely mature dog who loved to stay and got on with everyone. Christmas morning would see the children in bed opening presents. Jake would also be in bed with us opening his present, which was always a large bone named, for some reason, the postman's leg. Snow or no snow we always walked Jake as a family before Christmas dinner, just like the films. Sadly Jake went the way of all flesh and along came Ollie. Ollie was from the same breeder and identical in every way, brown coat eyes and nose.

Ollie although looking like Jake was quite different in character, he had a *Peter Pan* approach to life. On a walk once somebody asked me how old Ollie was. It was embarrassing to say seven as the man thought he was still a puppy because of his antics. The reason for Ollie's behaviour was I'm sure the house he came from. The husband would go to work early and as such made no fuss of Ollie for fear of waking up the household. His two daughters however would awake to treat Ollie as a living doll. Subsequently first thing in the morning Ollie would be all over you like a rash for at least half an hour. I know this time frame well as it's the length of time needed before you could safely hold a cup of tea in your hand or sit on the toilet without Ollie's head being between your legs or paws tightly round the back of your neck.

Ollie also had other issues regarding himself. He couldn't stand the thought of being ignored and would be in your face straight away. This idea of self importance would often manifest itself into jealousy. One of the many instances of jealousy was dancing with my wife in the front room. Ollie started low and wriggled himself between us until he was dancing with us. If my wife and I were to sit on the settee together Ollie would sit between us. On one memorable occasion whilst talking to my wife on the settee Ollie stood up and looking my wife directly in the eye started to move his back-end towards my head. After a minute Ollie's backside was firmly pressed against my mouth preventing me from speaking. This may have been a critic of what I was saying or an attempt to stop me speaking to anyone other than him, he never said so we don't know.

Ollie was often referred to as the pest because of his antic indoors and his habit of pestering other dogs on walks. Never having been hurt Ollie was confident and eager to play tag. The only dogs that could live with Ollie's speed were greyhounds and they were a spent force within four minutes whereas Ollie being a gun dog could run all day.

Ollie the pest seemed to be the nickname Ollie would always be stuck with until he showed his true colours and became Ollie the hero. Boxing day at 4 am. Ollie barked. Ollie never barks unless he deems it very important. Thinking we had over indulged Ollie with his Christmas dinner my wife (my poor wife always gets the nocturnal toilets) got up to toilet him. Upon reaching the back door Angela could see through the gloom a man trying to break into next door's garage which was two hundred feet away. My wife immediately woke me and I loosed Ollie out the back door hoping he would at least get the back out of the burglar's trousers. Ollie's fast but with a 200-foot head start the burglar managed to scramble over the back fence before impact. We later found out two garages in the next street had been burgled that same night. I don't think my neighbour, who's not particularly a dog person, believed Ollie had saved his property. However the neighbour never again referred "jokingly" to the noise of dogs barking in my house or garden again.

On a subsequent visit Ollie jumped up to show affection to Angela with a full dog hug. Unknown to man or beast the unsteadying of Angela's ample but perfect derrière had managed to turn on a gas ring. Whilst Angela took Ollie for a walk I was upstairs playing with the magic box (computer). Upon the happy couple's return from their walk the whole of downstairs was filled with gas! The lesson to be learned here is not to walk downstairs lighting a pipe until you're sure the house is gas free. Fortunately for me on this occasion I didn't go downstairs which is why I and the house are still here. The subsequent debate of who nearly blew who up found Ollie to be entirely blameless.

Ollie's ability to spot and alert you to trouble was now set. A man had been observed in the woods hiding behind trees dressed all in black and taking a somewhat unhealthy interest in schoolgirls and women. Word of a wrong'un being about soon spread, even the police sent a few officers around from time to time.

My wife took Ollie for his morning walk through the woods on her own. Being on her own was of course the day the man in black was about. Swaggering towards my wife the man in black was suddenly confronted by Ollie who made it very clear that the man wasn't going anywhere near my wife by his insistent barking. Ollie had double treats that day for his brave loyalty.

My wife reported the incident to the police. The officer concerned probably had a mother but no father. When my wife informed the officer "even the dog knew he was a wrong'un". The officers sad reply was the dog wouldn't make a good witness on the stand! This story is yet (I suspect) to run its full course. Ollie the hero, how much I love and owe him.

Dobermans are not your typical man's best friend or at least they look that way. Apart from the obvious fruit cakes all dogs respond to nurture, i.e. how they're treated and educated. Not dissimilar from humans then. The poor Doberman had half her back foot sliced off running over broken glass on a common. Despite all efforts the wound never properly healed. The Doberman never complained and walked normally. It was only off the lead that it became apparent she had a problem as she would run on three legs holding the injured back leg high off the ground. Even this didn't hold her back as she ran almost as fast on three pegs as four. The only difficulty seemed to be other dog walkers constantly reporting to me that the dog must have just broken her leg.

As intimated earlier most dog lovers are quite intimidated by Dobermans and other dogs don't seem keen either especially one firing on just three pots. This Doberman like so many others was lovely and if anything too affectionate. Between three and four every morning she would jump on to the bed to check that I was still there and wasn't dead. Not many people I trust have been woken in the early hours with a Doberman nose against theirs and a Doberman tongue licking their throat. Scary, yes but hey in time you get used to anything.

I had occasion to dog walk for a magistrate whilst she was in court. I held her house keys for a number of years, trust indeed. Her three collies were a mixed bunch. One had three legs and was always at the front door first but wasn't allowed out for walks. If looks could kill as I took the other two out. The second oldest collie was Barney and he was stone deaf and always had to be woken on the upstairs bed to go out for a walk. Shep was the youngest and was unusual in being free of any handicap. On walks Shep would often round up Barney and bring him back after he'd lost sight of our change of direction. Eventually I realised that deaf Barney could sign and believed the magistrate had instigated this, not so, it was the rapport between me and the dog. If I changed direction I would make sure Barney saw me point and to the direction I was about to go in.

Signing to Barney had it's downside as people often failed to see Barney but always spotted a shabby dressed man (dog walking clothes are not the height of fashion) in the undergrowth making strange gestures. This culminated on a walk in beckoning Barney to me and pointing to the track through the undergrowth I was about to take. Unfortunately two young schoolgirls who I was oblivious to were between me and Barney. They perceived my actions to be that of a wrong'un and were caught between having to admit they were hopping the wag and phoning the police. As the two "little darlings" reached for their guns (mobile phones) I called out that the dog behind them was deaf and I was signing to him. The girls turned around to see Barney and after a joint "Ah Bless" offered to help walk my disabled dogs and replaced their guns back into their holsters. After that incident I always made a point of speaking when signing to escape any misunderstanding and prevent me from writing this book from a very dark place.

Eventually the magistrate's three dogs passed on but I still had the same arrangement with her son at his house. He had a collie as well which needed so much ball throwing I purchased a tennis racket to save the ball joint in my shoulder. It didn't work, the ball went further but the collie never tired of retrieving it. Eventually a staff pup was added to the family as company for the collie. This brings me to a low point with dog care as the collie and staff stayed for a week. The collie was OK but the staff if left for five minutes was very destructive. Digging out the foam from the front room suite brought my wife to the brink and she declared no more dogs in this house! I couldn't find fault with her logic but faced a bleak future being dog-less. One swallow doth not a summer make and my wife eventually came around to realizing not every dog digs out the front room furniture.

The beasty boys were two Rottweiler-Alsatian crosses and fully grown but only eight months old. They had the dexterity and look of Rottweilers and the brains of Alsatians. Fearsome to look at but very people and dog friendly. People and dogs seemed unaware of this fact and quickly moved away as the beasty boys came to town. Mind you seeing two Rottweilers galloping towards you can have that effect especially as they hadn't yet discovered brakes as my wife can testify. The language of my wife was not lady like after picking herself up yet again from sodden grass after the beasty boys had made yet another "I'm so pleased to see you" charge.

In truth my house was too small for them, it wouldn't have been if they hadn't used it as a playpen. The brothers took particular pleasure in play fighting in the front room, showing off their prowess. Unfortunately hitting a coffee table with their backsides had no feeling on them until the table hit the television. The point of this episode is beer money yes but there's no real profit in looking after dogs at home.

Torra is a Shiba Inu, they're rare but in essence a miniature husky from Japan (the Japsanese like everything small). Torra's first owner was a youngish woman who was wheelchair bound through polio. Eventually the elderly mother took over dog care when the daughter died. Lets face it the dog had little chance of having extensive walks and so had developed a dread of the outside world including gardens. Only the urgency of the toilet would necessitate a short outside visit. All dogs I've had with one exception have strained to get through the front door as soon as their lead is touched. The one exception was a sheep dog who would lay down as soon you reached the end of the front path. She would run all day in the back garden but would not put a paw onto pavement.

Torra was so adamant about the big outside she would run and hide under the bed as soon as her lead was touched.

If you managed to put Torra on her choke lead she would shake her head and walk backwards and escape. It didn't help that Torra's neck was bigger than her head. Once free Torra would run back home so you had to keep her choke lead very tight as in Crufts. We balanced Torra's unwillingness to exercise outside by getting down on all fours and chasing her from room to room for half an hour twice a day. This seemed enough for Torra as she quickly fell asleep afterwards. The only problem for us was housemaid's knee which often lead to an early curtailment of the chasing game.

It never ceases to amaze me how close people can become to their dogs and I expect animals in general. Polo and Tia are two Schnauzers who were very much loved by their owners. Polo the husband (thank god he was a boy otherwise he'd have been called Maria), was twice the size of Tia his wife and very protective of her. On their first stay Polo was very suspicious of me and kept his distance. Tia on the other hand went for alpha male and would often sleep on my lap. After a few days Polo replaced Tia on my lap and never left my side thereafter. Whatever room I was in Polo was in. I took a forgotten toy back to Polo and Tia's house one day and their owner greeted me and let me in. After a few minutes the husband turned to his wife and said "why are the dogs not barking".

Her reply didn't altogether please her husband as she said "it's Graham".

"But the dogs bark at all the family" he replied.

"They love Graham" his wife replied. Looking at the husband's cuckold face I thought it'll be the last I see of Polo and Tia! Not so we had them many times over the years and our families became close friends.

After time the dogs' health suffered due to age, Polo in particular. Having suffered a fit or stroke he was taken to a veterinary college in Hertfordshire for treatment and a brain scan. This type of treatment cost thousands of pounds and of course was not covered by pet insurance. Polo's owners never flinched and paid whatever it took to patch Polo up. As long as the dog had a quality of life they were prepared to pay any amount.

Whilst being taught by dogs the intricacies of the canine world I've also learnt how to socialize with people from different sexes (all three of them) and socio-economic backgrounds. Pip's owner had obviously been to a public school and spoke perfect BBC English. My wife (non BBC English) upon calling Pip's owner Charlie and was promptly corrected to Charles. Charles (ninety-odd) was off to a dirty weekend of ballroom dancing on the south coast with a young lady (eighty-five). Before he left he warned us Pip had led a sheltered life and was not used to the ladies.

Pip fitted in very well, he had terrible wind and snoring problems but for an old Jack Russell was otherwise normal. Pip had full run of the house but one day fell down the stairs, he walked across the front room into a chair. Walking like a drunk Pip made it to the garden walked into a fence and fell down, he got up cocked his leg and fell down again. I picked Pip up and convinced he was dying placed him in his bed so he could die in peace. A short while later Pip was missing from his bed, I searched the whole house, no Pip. I found Pip at the bottom of the garden with all four legs in the air, if it hadn't been for the snoring I'd have said the dog was dead. It was only some time afterwards that I found out one of my son's friends had stashed some cannabis under my son's bed and Pip had eaten it. Far from heading to the elephant's graveyard, Pip had been as high as a kite. This would have been difficult to explain to Charlie, sorry Charles so we kept quiet. The funny thing was on Pip's next visit he made straight for my son's bedroom to get another fix. Charles was always surprised at the enthusiasm Pip showed when approaching our house!

Looking after dogs is not as easy as it sounds. Apart from the responsibility it can take you to places law-abiding citizens would not normally experience. Sapphi and Bella came to stay and were perfectly okay until the night I was late to bed. Sapphi always slept upstairs on my wife's side of the bed. Upon entering the bedroom I detect all was not well aroma wise. Within two steps my foot had found the source. Hopping around the bedroom floor trying to find the light switch I called out "you dirty bitch, you cow". Sapphi knowing what she'd done and not knowing I wouldn't hurt her legged it bang bang bang downstairs. All the house lights went on as I erased all evidence of Sapphi's crime.

The next-door neighbour who is also chairman of the local neighbourhood watch called to me the next day over the garden fence. After a brief conversation about what had happened the night before it was apparent that the neighbour thought my words were directed at my wife and she had fled downstairs before I could give her a whack! You wouldn't think looking after a dogs could get you arrested for wife beating, but it very nearly happened.

Hercules wasn't at first what his name suggested being a small Border Terrier. However the operative word here is terrier and Hercules was not going to be threatened or knocked about without serious input. I took Hercules to the pub one day and tied him to a garden table whilst I went to the bar. Suddenly a loud crash and upon turning around I could see the dog had dragged not only the table but also a chair into the pub in order to see what I was doing. I gathered the now-frightened dog into my arms in order to calm him. The pub owners rushed to my aid and declared how strong the little dog was and enquired as to his name! It was with trepidation I announced Hercules in fear I would be thought to be extracting the urine.

Hercules could have off days when small dog syndrome could take over. He stayed with me one day but on his short journey up the garden path missed a cat taking shelter under our car. Frustrated all morning Hercules was not happy. On his lunchtime walk he was approached by two dogs upon which he vented his displeasure. One dog running free legit, the second dog on an extension lead tied my ankles together in his attempt to escape. Acting under the forces of gravity I found myself flat on my back. This in itself was bad enough but in my clutching-at-straws reaction managed to burst the dog's mess bag which until then I'd managed to keep intact. I was covered in it all for the sake of a missed-cat opportunity.

All dogs become our dogs during their stay but some more than others. Roxy was an eight-month-old Labrador and stayed with us for four months. The owners went on a world cruise and wished the cruise opportunity had come before they acquired the dog. Roxy had never been let off the lead before so once she fixed on us we let her off. I've rarely seen a dog so happy running free. The problem was she was unable to deal with anything on four legs. Having been kept on the lead and caged from time to time Roxy was very short on confidence. Angela and myself are dog liberals and Roxy became over confident. Very soon she realized that being on furniture, going in the river, sleeping upstairs by the bed and sniffing the backs of other dogs was quite normal. Upon Roxy's first moult the front room carpet turned black (black Labrador), black hair covered everything to the extent you would constantly wipe your face as if you had walked into spiders' webs. A five minute vacuum of the front room would fill two container of the vacuum cleaner. In fact it appeared that more dog hair had gone up the vacuum cleaner than was on the dog.

After being with us for four months and having suffered such a liberal regime Angela and I became very concerned as to how Roxy would react to going back home. We needn't have worried Roxy fitted straight back into her old behaviour pattens, Labradors are clumsy but clever.

Upon Roxy's penultimate day staying with us she ripped the seat cushion on her favourite armchair. It could have been vengeance or retaliation for having to leave the next day otherwise why wait four months to become a vandal. Who knows the true workings of a dog's mind? I scolded Roxy for the damage and she was suitably humbled. In fact she looked as if physical punishment would have been preferable to a raised voice from me.

To sum up it's been an honour and privilege to have looked after so many dogs and been introduced to their owners. The warm feeling of pleasure when a dog greets us or pulls their owner inside the house is priceless. At times I've felt like I should be paying the owners because of the joy and interest their pets give us. Most of the kids (dogs) we've looked after aren't mentioned because their stays were relatively event free.

The main curiosity for me is the number of dogs who send us postcards advising they arrived home safely and are keeping well and can't wait for the next holiday. Many greeting cards at Christmas from dogs is not uncommon. The puzzling thing is when the dogs stayed they never, I mean never let on they could read and write.

Without a dog in the house Angela and I are like fish out of water, it's like the children have grown and left home so we pass the time reminiscing on past and future dog visits. The writing of this book has been done during periods of doglessness and is really an attempt to exorcize the empty feeling we have without our canine mates in the house.